This book is dedicated to my husband, Mike, who has taken me to many National Parks and helped me to see the beauty in nature.

A Close Up Look at

Sequoia National Park

By Josie Zayac

At Sequoia National Park

you'll find the largest trees.

You must go and visit.

Ask your parents, please!

Take a close look.

What do you see?

I see a jimson weed

as pretty as can be.

Take a close look.

What do you see?

The leaves of a fern . . .

. . . and branches of a tree.

Take a close look.

What do you see?

It is a pinecone that has fallen from a tree.

Take a close look. What do you see?

Is it a flower? No, just a weed.

Take a close look.

What do you see?

The forest floor . . .

. . . and the bark of a tree.

Take a close look.

What do you see?

Lichen growing on a sequoia tree.

Take a close look.

What do you see?

Yuck! It's trash,

lying next to a tree.

Who would do that?

Not you and not me.

Take a close look.

What do you see?

The rings telling the age

of a cut-down tree.

Take a close look.

What do you see?

It's a horsetail, but no horse do I see.

Take a close look.

What do you see?

A clump of needles

fallen from a tree.

Take a close look.

What do you see?

Common fiddleneck,

for you and for me!

Take a close look.

What do you see?

There's so much more

than mountains and trees.

Go out and explore,

take a look at some bark.

And remember to

protect our precious park.

Facts about Sequoia National Park, California

- John Muir, conservationist, explored and named the forest
- It is the second oldest National Park (Yellowstone is the oldest)
- Sequoias grow on the west side of the Sierra Nevada Mountain Range
- No tree is bigger in mass than General Sherman giant sequoia tree
- It stands 275 feet tall and weighs 1,385 tons, circumference is 103 feet

Look for other National Park books by Dr. Josie Zayac

- A Close Up Look at Bryce Canyon National Park
- A Close Up Look at Crater Lake National Park
- A Close Up Look at Cuyahoga Valley National Park
- A Close Up Look at Joshua Tree National Park
- A Close Up Look at Redwood National and State Parks
- A Close Up Look at Rocky Mountain National Park
- A Close Up Look at Sequoia National Park
- A Close Up Look at Theodore Roosevelt National Park
- A Close Up Look at Zion National Park

www.ingramcontent.com/pod-product-compliance
Lightning Source LLC
Chambersburg PA
CBHW050930290526
45792CB00002B/954